Blended Hearts

Blended Hearts

Angie Johnson

Copyright

The story 'Blended Hearts' is a work of fiction *inspired* by actual events. Names, characters, businesses, places, events, incidents and dialogue are drawn from the author's imagination and are not to be construed as real. Any resemblance to actual events or persons, living or dead, is entirely coincidental.

Copyright © 2016 by **Angela Johnson**. All rights reserved. This book or any portion thereof may not be reproduced or used in any manner whatsoever without the express written permission of Angela Johnson except for the use of brief quotations in a book review.

Printed in the United States of America

First Printing, 2016

ISBN-13: 978-1-942022-62-6

ISBN10: 194202262X

The Butterfly Typeface Publishing
PO BOX 56193
Little Rock Arkansas 72215

Dedication

I dedicate this book to my husband David, for all his patience, kind words, support and love. I love you and I pray that this will get better.

I also dedicate this book to all who have gone through or maybe are going through something similar. May you find some comfort in knowing that you are not alone. I pray for peace for you as well.

"When you feel like giving up, remember why you held on so long in the first place."

-unknown

Table of Contents

Give Love	17
Changed Forever	21
Living The Aftermath	26
Only God Knows	36
A Rock and a Hard Place	45
Bitter Baby Mamas	55
An Inconvenience	61
Forever Grateful	68
Past the Bitterness	76
Blurred Lines	82
God Had Other Plans	90
Like Nothing Happened	95
A Bigger Issue	99
Food for Thought	104

Epilogue

Book Club Discussions

About the Author

Foreword

What is it like to be married and blend a family? Having a child and marrying a man who also had a child qualifies Angie Johnson to help us understand the impact the struggles a 'ready-made-family' can have on your marriage.

I am proud of my cousin/friend for shedding light on this issue with her story *Blended Hearts*. I can relate to some of the difficulties because I also have a blended family that I love very much. My husband and I have been together 20 years and married for 17 of them.

With a love for God, her husband and children, Angie fought for her marriage, which inspired *Blended Hearts* to be written.

Angie and her husband David have known each other for more than 30 years and together have overcome a lot of obstacles that were facing their marriage and have blossomed into a blessed, beautiful couple.

I really love this couple and I'm glad to know that in spite of their trials and tribulations, with God's help and their faith, they fought and won their marriage.

For anyone who is struggling with their blended family, this book can be a help to you.

Andrea Williams

Director
Chosen Ones
Child Development Center

Acknowledgments

Blended Hearts was written from the depths of my heart. It was written over the years through many ups and downs that my entire family experienced.

Because of these experiences we have been forever changed. I Thank God for keeping me! Only God knows what these changes may bring about for our future. There are so many that have encouraged me to be patient and listened as I just cried - sometimes with no words.

A big thanks to my loving husband, David. Through thick and thin, ups and down, we always managed to never ever go to bed angry. We always managed to work that thing through.

I want to thank everyone that welcomed each of our children as MINE and never treated them any differently regardless as to what I was going through. I want to thank my parents for being excellent parents and extraordinary grandparents to all of their grandchildren.

I can't forget Detra Harris, your love, advice and support has been invaluable. A special thanks to Dre for being mommy's forever understanding *lil man* and LeLee my ray of sunshine!

Dre you have grown into such a handsome responsible young adult and father. LeLee you have grown into a beautiful teenager.

A big thank you to Angel Starks for giving me that extra push I really needed to get started.

Thank you to Iris M. Williams for believing in me and pulling out of me what I was scared to share. Thank you for welcoming me into your company, *The Butterfly Typeface Publishing*.

This book is my story...it may be your story.

Blended Hearts highlights the hardships caused within the marriage of James and Faith by his daughter Janiece's mom, Monica. Faith felt that Monica was intentionally causing havoc because she truly wanted a relationship with her child's father.

James chose to move on, but he didn't realize that moving on would mean causing his daughter Janiece pain and torment. He also didn't realize that he would be putting so many others at risk.

Blended Hearts focuses on the pain, torture and unimaginable suffering one couple experienced while trying to blend their families.

This is one woman's account of what can happen to a couple when the ex refuses to let go ...

Give Love

> "Family is not an important thing,
> it is everything."
> **-Michael J. Fox**

Growing up, family was everything to me – it still is. Love was beautiful and seemed an effortless thing in my immediate family. So you can imagine my surprise that *blending* a family wouldn't be just as easy. I figured as long as I had love in my heart and an open mind that everything would simply fall into place. Boy was I in for a rude awakening.

Now don't get me wrong, I still believe in love and family - but blending a family is very hard and a constant struggle. Blending is taking two or more things and combining them together as one so that others cannot tell them apart. In my quest to blend my family as one I met more challenges than the law should allow any one person to bear. I have felt mentally, physically and emotionally broken on so many occasions that I questioned myself and even my marriage throughout the journey.

I grew up in a household with both parents, an older brother and a younger sister. Thinking back now, I had an awesome childhood complete with two parents who loved us kids and protected us from harm to the best of their abilities. I can never remember a time hearing my parents argue, let alone put one another down. We sat down at the dinner table together and when time allowed we did the same for breakfast. I cherished those times and knew that these would be things that I would do within my family someday.

When you are young you take many things for granted, but as you grow older you learn to appreciate some of the smaller things. Trust me I now appreciate even the smallest dinner time conversations shared with my parents. I appreciate never hearing my parents argue or fight. I appreciate my parents showing me what parenting was and not just going through the motions. I appreciate the love that was showered upon us kids unconditionally. We were given respect so we knew how to give respect. We were shown love, so we knew how to *give love.*

Angie Johnson

Changed Forever

"Having somewhere to go is home.
Having someone to love is family.
Having both is a blessing."
-Author Unknown

I met my husband James, when I was thirteen years old while visiting the local skating rink with my best friend. He was seventeen and so my best friend and I were kids to him and his friends, but eventually we all became friends. They seemed to genuinely look out for us. Over the years we always kept in touch and remained friends, talking and even visiting one another from time to time. I remember at one point I was in Beauty College and he came in and let me give him a Jerry Curl. Now that's a friend - I needed that to pass the course! I remember thinking, "I love this man!" He wasn't even my husband at the time.

While James and I were still just friends, I had my handsome son Jason in 1991 and in 1994 James had a beautiful daughter named Janiece with a young lady from

Illinois. Janiece was the apple of her daddy's eye! From the start, James was a good father to his children. No one ever had to ask him for anything. The kids always had what they needed and more – this included Janiece's siblings who were not fathered by James.

Early on, our two children knew each other and played well together for the most part, that is until Janiece's Mom, Monica, realized that James and I were starting a relationship.

James moved in with me and that's when Monica realized just how serious things were with us. She started blocking his attempts to bring Janiece to our home.

"You are NOT going to play momma with my child," she'd say to me with such hatred. When she couldn't rattle me, she'd start in on James.

"I don't want her combing Janiece's hair!"

James didn't let that deter him from his life with me so she decided that he couldn't take Janiece from her home. She even went as far as to say that Janiece needed to see her and James together. When she insisted that he couldn't see Janice outside of her home, that's when James has finally had enough. He and I both knew it was time to get the courts involved because Monica was not going to be reasonable.

Starting a romantic, long term relationship with James was a game changer in the whole dynamics of our blended family efforts. *My entire world and how things really worked was about to be changed forever!*

Angie Johnson

Living The Aftermath

"I sustain myself with love and family."
-Maya Angelou

Before we got married, James started bringing Janiece to my house for short day visits when she was about three and half maybe four years old. The visits were fine. The kids played well together. Jason loved having a little sister and she loved having a big brother. Janiece seemed to absolutely adore me and I felt the same towards her. I had always wanted a large family. (To this day my house is the house where everyone drops their kids off - need a babysitter, Faith got you, lol!)

Blending seemed to be happening naturally – until it wasn't. Somewhere, we caught a snag. Monica started playing on my phone and giving James a hard time about getting Janiece. She even began telling me how my relationship would play out...

"Honey, James has always told me that he will NEVER settle down," she shouted. "I know yo prissy a** ain't gonna put up with the stuff I have so you may as well save yourself the aggravation and walk away now. If you don't, trust me – you will regret it!"

Monica was a woman obsessed. I didn't think this type of stuff existed. I read about bitter women and even saw some TV shows, but I really thought that stuff was a little exaggerated. I shrugged my shoulders and figured it would all blow over soon. I was so wrong.

She warned me. "As long as I have a child with James, I'll make sure your life is a living hell."

That's exactly what she set out to do. I believe whole heartedly that she was behind all the phone calls from people calling me names, telling me to walk away and let him be a father to his child and even later in the relationship when one of her children called and told me to quit playing momma to Janiece. Monica's bitterness spilled over to her children who I had done absolutely nothing to.

Monica played on my phone so much and called all the shots with James seeing Janiece that I felt like I was losing my mind. She finally told James the only time he could see his daughter would be at her house and that he was not allowed to take the child anywhere.

"Really James? You are paying child support for your child and doing everything else for her so why do you have to ask permission to see her?"

James did not know how to go about petitioning the courts for certain rights and neither did I. So I did some research and drew up the petition for him to have certain parental rights. By the Grace and Mercy of God it was granted! Now before you start clapping for James's triumph, please know that the devil stays busy!

I did my best to make sure that Janiece never felt that she didn't belong in our home. We remodeled so that she'd have her own room and a *full wardrobe* there as well! Monica never had to pack one single thing for Janiece when she came over. I went overboard to be accommodating and it seemed Monica went overboard showing me how my attempts meant nothing to her.

She took every opportunity she could to clown me – including in court.

"Why in the *hell* is she here James?" She hissed with venom.

I thought if she rolled her eyes at me any harder, she'd probably fall asleep! Neither James nor I responded which only made her angrier.

"What are you trying to prove? *She* has nothing to do with what goes on between *us* and *our* child!" She insisted.

When she realized that she was not going to get a rise out of me, she went there with James, but he too refused to let her 'take him there' and we both managed to stay calm. When her attempts to make a scene in court didn't work, she decided to go another route - through her own child.

During visitation pickups and drop offs she would clown and attempt to start arguments by not answering the door for long periods of time or sending snotty messages for me through Janiece. During this time, Janiece started behaving very disrespectful towards me. She would tell me things like, "I don't have to listen to you. You ain't my momma."

She would start intentionally being destructive and when we asked, she told us blatantly that her momma told her to do certain things.

Janiece wanted to call me what my son Jason was calling me and she felt comfortable doing so. So she'd consistently call me Momma regardless of what her mom said except when she thought her mom could hear her. I understood why Janiece behaved this way. If she liked me, she would get into trouble with her mom. This is why whenever Monica was in hearing range; I went from being *Momma* to *Faith*

Fridays were the hardest because her behavior would be all about what she was programmed to say and or do by her mom during the week prior. However, by Saturday, she would be stuck to me like glue, calling me momma and wanting to do everything I did and go everywhere I went. Really? I was like now you *just* treated me like crap yesterday, but today if I bent over you would fall out of my behind. Lol.

We loved each other and I knew she was torn because her mom was teaching her against me. By Sunday this child was a complete mess.

"I don't want to go home Momma," Janiece cried. "Mom is going to be mad because I was here and I let you comb my hair!"

Sounds stupid I know! But I lived this. As a matter of fact, I am still *living the aftermath.*

Angie Johnson

Only God Knows

"Families are messy.
Immortal families are eternally messy.
Sometimes the best we can do
is remind each other that we're related
for better or worse...
and try to keep the maiming and killing
to a minimum."
-Rick Riordan

There is so much that goes on behind the scenes that most never know about. Whether you call it your *dirty little secret* or *dirty laundry*, the bottom line is that you never really want anyone to know. You think if you keep it to yourself that maybe it will work itself out or possibly even go away. This wasn't true for us.

When Janiece began her court ordered visitations, I soon realized that there were vast differences in the household her mom was running and the household I was running. There were also differences in what James allowed from Janiece verses Jason and what I would allow. Janiece wasn't use to having to sit down at the dinner table to eat a meal. While we all usually ate as family, she was accustomed to being able to walk around as she ate or drank. She would want to put everything away in my refrigerator saying, "I don't want the bugs to get in it." Before I could get offended, James explained to me that they had bugs really bad and that is what they did over there.

We ran a tight ship. Jason wouldn't dare think or dream of disrespecting me. When Jason's tone wasn't right James stepped right in to correct him, but not with Janiece. Janiece didn't respect the rules and wasn't expected to because she was the baby. In my eyes, even the baby had to learn the rules. I tried (and trust me I really did try) to allow James the space to do the disciplining because I did not want *that* fight on my hand. But Janiece ruled the nest with her puppy dog eyes, sniffles and her "but my momma routine" and James always gave passes.

On the one hand I truly felt sorry for Janiece, but on the other I had feelings too and they were being hurt, stepped on and crushed by not only Monica, but by Janiece as well and now I was being pushed aside by my husband. I understood that on many occasions James felt like he needed to just let her slide because she was only there for the weekend, but I was afraid that we were sending the wrong message to Jason. Our son was learning that Janiece could disrespect us with no real consequences.

Monica would never say outright to James that I abused Janiece, but she did insinuate that he didn't know what I do to Janiece when he wasn't around. He'd ask her what she was talking about and she'd flip the tables and say, "You just believe anything your wifey says so what does it matter what I say." It was always something with her.

Janiece would come home upset about this or that and say something about 'your wife', but when questioned further, she would not elaborate or anything. It was just a way to cause division between James and I. This would happen on occasions when unbeknownst to Monica, James was home the entire time Janiece was there. Monica figured Janiece was home with only me and saw it as an opportunity to get a rise out of James.

This sickened me. If for one minute my husband would have bought into her abuse allegations, there is no telling what could have happened to me. I have never and would never do anything to harm any of my children (Janiece is my child) or anyone else's child for that matter.

Things had gotten so bad that at one point I began to get physically sick nearly every time it was time to pick her up. I would never say anything. I just endured it, put a smile on my face and prayed that *this too would pass.*

"No one can be this evil for this long," I rationalized. "This has to pass soon."

I was praying that she would find her a fine, handsome man that would sweep her off her feet and take care of her and she would stop all the torment of James and our family.

This whole situation was so embarrassing. Often I felt that I had no one that I could talk to about what was going on. I loved this child even though she totally disrespected me at every turn. Most of the time it seemed like my husband knew she was wrong, but defended her just to have her by his side and that irked my soul! Her mom called me every name in the book except a child of God, yet I had never said one bad word against her or even to her.

This was tearing me down and in so many ways it continues to because my husband still doesn't have the relationship he deserves or wants with his daughter. I kept encouraging him to not give up on his child. I also reminded him that she would get older and realize that he tried; she would get older and know that he was there. She would have her memories. But you know what? That is not always true. I guess time will tell. *Only God knows.*

Angie Johnson

A Rock and a Hard Place

"You may not control all the events that happen to you, but you can decide not to be reduced by them."
-Mahatma Gandhi

In the fall of 1999, James and I were excited to learn that we were expecting. We were excited about our newest addition to our family, but we chose not to share the news right away. We were nervous for several reasons; one being my health, two the dynamics of Monica and Janiece and three, you're always nervous when you are expanding your family. However, aside from all of that I was super excited because as I said earlier, I had always wanted a large family. About two and a half months into the pregnancy, we started telling our family and close friends. Things became more real.

"James, we are really expanding our family," I said with excitement.

"Now Janiece is going to have someone to boss around," I laughed. "She'll be someone's big sister."

Somewhere in late March of 2000 I started to show my pregnancy. Not that I really was hiding it, but we both knew that it was going to be a huge issue with Janiece's mom and so we wanted to avoid it as long as possible. To our relief things were relatively quiet for the most part until I got closer to the end of my term.

Both Jason and Janiece seemed happy about having a little sister to welcome home soon. Then one day out of the blue Janiece blindsides me.

"That baby in your belly is not my Daddy's baby!"

Wow! I was in disbelief. How could a six-year-old say something so harsh and with such conviction. I was hurt.

"Janiece, why would you say such a thing."

"My Momma said it's not and that I'm my Daddy's only child."

"What," I was so shocked I couldn't seem to comprehend her words at first.

"Yep," she happily explained. "…and she said that Jason is not my brother and she told me she'd better not hear me saying it again."

I knew in my heart that this woman wanted her child to be James's only child and that she really wanted him to settle down with her. She really truly meant for me to walk away. Our baby was just further proof that her desires just weren't' going to happen. I knew she was angry, but I didn't think it the realization that she didn't know any better.

Janelle came home and added new dimensions to James' stress with Janiece. Monica accused him of not wanting Janiece anymore since he had a new family and a new daughter. She accused him of no longer having time even though he stuck to his court appointed arrangements and would have gladly taken more if she'd have allowed it.

Monica hated James' new addition and she shared this with Janiece and Janiece was all too happy to share this information with us. It was hurtful, but there was nothing we could do. We couldn't make her like us or our children. So we just tried to discourage Janiece from saying hateful things about Janelle, Jason or myself when she was at our house.

We would often try to do little outings while Janiece was over and when we were out the kids would usually be dressed similar. Janiece got a kick out of this, so I'm going to go as far as to say that she must have shared her enthusiasm with her mother. That didn't go over well.

"B****," Monica yelled into the phone. "Don't you be playing dress up with my d*** kid!"

Now that was some mess in my opinion. Parents often dress their kids alike or similar. I considered Janiece apart of our family so what was the harm in doing what parents do? Monica was just over the top with her madness and this type of stuff let me know there was no end to what she may or may not do. She was just petty.

Janelle was growing up confused with her siblings. The kids loved one another and Janelle was so young, all she knew and wanted was her big sister Janiece.

As a mother it was my job to protect her when I saw things that weren't right. All of the kids were being hurt and I felt powerless to help. I was caught in between

a rock and a hard place.

Bitter Baby Mamas

"Let no man pull you so low as to hate him."
-Martin Luther King Jr.

I remember Janiece's graduation from kindergarten like it was yesterday. Everyone knows that this is a major milestone in a child's lifetime as well as for the parent. Because of her past actions, Monica's reaction to me attending the ceremony wasn't really a shocker. She decided to create more drama and called James on the telephone:

"The school is not allowing any outsiders to attend our child's graduation, so you can't bring your little wifey."

James told me it wasn't so much what she said, but rather how she said it that bothered him. Well, I am not going to lie to you - it hurt me deeply. It was just more hurt to deal with and it was more clear to me that this woman didn't want me to exist at all. She wanted them to be seen together as a family – a family that didn't include me.

It didn't' matter to her that he had decided to move on. It didn't matter to her that I hadn't held a gun to his head and forced him to leave. It didn't seem to matter to her that many people, including Janiece, were being hurt by her bitterness. And it definitely didn't matter to her that I had done nothing, but love her child.

When I married James, I took on his daughter as well. Who did she think took care of her baby when she came over to our home? When her hair is looking all pretty, she's dressed all nice and dolled up - that's all me! When she is sick and needs medicine or just her tummy or back rubbed - that was me too! I loved that little girl as my own and still do. So, I was going to that graduation in support of my child, not just my husband.

Anyway, I ended up calling the school myself to find out the information about the graduation and guess what? They welcomed everyone! Yes, everyone. The principal said that so many times no one shows so they extend it to everyone to show support for their babies.

We showed up to the graduation with bells on! As we made our way inside, I remember being excited, but nervous as well. I wasn't sure what would 'pop off' or what Monica may do. My stomach was a mess, but like always, I hid all of my emotions well and even managed to put a smile on my face. We walked into the auditorium and waved at our child and cheered her on as she walked across the stage. We got the entire graduation on video and took so many pictures you would have thought she was President Obama!

I could feel Monica's piercing stares and I knew that if her eyes had bullets, I would have been dead. I know she couldn't believe that he had the nerves to bring me when she distinctly told him, I wasn't allowed. No words were exchanged after the ceremony except for between us and Janiece to take pictures. I thought that it was truly sad. If given the opportunity, I probably would have spoken to her, but she walked away so quickly as if to say, "Don't even try it!"

I'll never understand all the bitterness when at this point we should be able to get along. I had done nothing, but love Janiece since day one. These *bitter baby mommas* just don't understand!

An Inconvenience

"People fail to get along because they fear each other. They fear each other because they don't know each other; they don't know each other because they have not communicated with each other."
-Martin Luther King Jr.

Our family vacations are great times. We usually included my brother, his family and my parents. When we start to plan the vacation we include Janiece and ask Monica about her going along. Now we are aware that sometimes this may conflict with her school schedules or whatever she and her mom may have planned for her which is why we give advance notice so it may be worked out if at all possible. This is just how it is when you have a blended family – you have to compromise.

Even with all of our effort, almost without fail Monica would flat out tell us NO right from the beginning, as if it didn't even warrant a consideration. Now don't get me wrong, I'm not saying because James wanted something she should have just given it to him. I'm just thinking it was at least worth consideration. Family and togetherness means a lot to me. If you start building your family memories when you are young, your family's foundation is much stronger and your love is much healthier, usually.

Angie Johnson

On the occasions that we managed to get Janiece on our family vacations it was always an ordeal. I can remember this one time we really wanted Janiece to go to *Lake of the Ozarks* with us. I mean we literally begged and was told no over and over again. We offered to shorten our stay by a day, suggested that she could get her school work in advance and promised we would make sure that she got it done. Janiece *really* wanted to go. But the answer was still no. None of that was as surprising as what came out of Janiece's own mouth.

"I can't go on vacation because you don't want me to go."

"Of course I want you to go," I explained. "I think you've misunderstood something."

"No, my momma told me that my daddy's wifey don't want me to go with yall." Janiece looked like she was on the verge of tears.

As you can imagine that floored me! I thought to myself, *what is this woman trying to do?* I told James about it and he got on the phone right then. Monica just laughed. *Who does this mess?* I could not believe this crap was happening and furthermore happening to me. We hadn't done anything wrong. We played by the rules. I took all of her abuse. This woman even allowed her older daughter to play on my phone and who knows who else.

Nothing was resolved from the conversation. We continued to ask about Janiece going to the Lake with us and Monica continued to say no. The day of our vacation arrived and it was a busy one with us packing the van and running last minute errands. In the midst of all this, the phone rings. It's Janiece.

"Hi baby," I greet her with my usual happy greeting.

"Hi Faith," I knew then that Monica was around. "Are you guys still going out of town?"

"Yes we are honey."

"Why don't you want me to go?"

"Janiece, that is not true," I'm fuming, but trying to remain calm. "I have asked your mother several times about you going and she has continued to tell us no."

Then I call James to the phone and give him a quick rundown about what is going on. He is pissed.

"James, you need to talk to them."

The bottom line is that we really wanted her to go. James gets on the phone with Monica and she finds the whole situation funny. In truth I think she knew all along she was going to let Janiece go, but it had to be on her terms. She was probably just going to see how long she could get us to beg and plead with her. Bottom line, Monica's mission all along seemed to have been to make our lives together *an inconvenience.*

Forever Grateful

"We must develop and maintain
the capacity to forgive.
He who is devoid
of the power to forgive,
is devoid of the power to love.
There is some good
in the worst of us,
and some evil in the best of us.
When we discover this, we are less prone
to hate our enemies."
-Martin Luther King Jr.

I ended up going to pick Janiece up while James finished preparing for our vacation. Monica knew I was in route, but she made me sit out there and just wait. I saw the kids looking out the window at me! I felt helpless and like a fool. The tears well up inside of me as I realized that she was making an even bigger fool of me right in front of her family. This was simply ridiculous. I mean this is the stuff that makes for good TV!

Janiece finally comes out and we are off. I am happy because we are going as a family. Janiece seems to be happy too. When Jason learned that his sister was coming with us he was happy as well.

As I am driving us back to our home, Janiece began coughing something horrible.

"Are you ok Janiece?" I ask full of concern.

"I've been sick for a while and I think I need my medicine," she replies between coughs.

WHAT!!! I am ready to just jump out of the car at this point. Did this child just say what I think she said? I stayed calm because this was just a child. It wasn't her fault if she was sick.

"Janiece honey, has your mommy been giving you medicine?"

"Yes," she coughs again. "Because I didn't go to school I had to take medicine."

Now I am really angry, but still I am trying my best to not show it. This woman is trying to sabotage my family's vacation. I get home and I tell James. We call Monica, but of course she doesn't answer the phone. She knows exactly what she is doing. I don't know any MOTHER who would do this. But I guess she figured since James is the other parent, he has to do his part in taking care of his sick child and since I am *wifey* as she says I must do my part as well.

We didn't have a problem with doing our part. We just didn't think it was fair that Monica got to decide when we could do it. James felt we should continue on with our plans since it seemed Janiece only had a cough. However, nearly two hours into our journey, I realize that Janiece also has a slight fever. After more questioning, she tells us that she had been taking medicine for that as well and had taken it when she woke up that morning. To me that was crazy to send your child away from home without really telling us what was going on with her. But that was ok, it proved to me that she knew deep down that we were all along providing excellent care for Janiece. She was still bitter that James moved on and settled down – without her.

We make it to our destination and I run out to the local Walmart to get the necessary medicines that I feel we are going to need for the duration of our trip. I get back and start to unpack. That's when I realized Janiece's bag is filled with damp clothes and too little shoes. Now what are we going to do with this?

I had already anticipated some foolery so we did prepack a few outfits and shoes for her, but this was ridiculous. What if we hadn't and what if we also didn't have the finances to afford to go and get this child anything while we were hundreds of miles away from home? I could never put *any* child through this, let alone my own child.

I really started getting the bigger picture at this point. Things were only going to get worse. Nothing was going to get better. She was not going to let up at all.

To add insult to injury, during this vacation, while nursing Janiece back to good health, Janelle and I both got sick too. I ended up having to spend one of our vacation days in the emergency room with Janelle. She had a fever over 102 that wouldn't go down and a cough. Wow, I wonder where that came from. The rest of the family enjoyed themselves for the most part. After about two days of rest, plenty of fluids and medicine, we enjoyed the remainder of the vacation too thankfully.

Long story short, Monica did manage to sour some parts of our vacation that time, but we got some good memories from it just the same (bonding time and great photos). For that we will be *forever grateful.*

Past the Bitterness

> "Being a family means you are part of something wonderful. It means you will love and be loved for the rest of your life."
> **-Lisa Weedn**

The headaches of seeing my husband drug back and forth to court over frivolous things were so stressful. It became so embarrassing and tiresome. It was almost routine to know that my husband was going to be in court at least once, twice or even three times a year concerning Janiece. I always encouraged my husband to see his daughter because I felt like every child needed a MAN in their life. James is a great father. He is not just a provider, but he is the kind of man who wants involvement in every aspect of his children's lives.

He was denied that opportunity with Janiece through harassment, hostility and aggravation. Even after he established court ordered visitations, she fought him on that and ordered him back to court saying she did not like the arrangements. (Because of his job, sometimes I would have to pick up or drop off Janiece to stay in compliance with the court order.) Monica only wanted him with Janiece and not his wife. The judge told her that this was *his* visitation time and that she could not dictate all that. He went on to say that I was James's wife, I represented him, and that she needed to get over it.

Then she started talking about child support and the judge explained to her that was something separate and that she needed to handle that in another court. He asked her if James was paying and she lied (The payments come directly out of his check!) and said no.

She left that court, went to where ever she needed to go to complain about child support and *then* we get papers pertaining to child support. We ended up back in court about child support. She kept saying she was not receiving her child support. In my opinion, that had nothing to do with

James. Because the payments were auto drafted, she gets her money before we see one red cent of James's money. Sure enough, the court looked it up and looked at the check stubs that James provided and sees that he had been paying and that because she was "on the system" she had to wait for them to do what they call distribution of their checks to the recipients. We also found out that not all of his payments went to her.

James has always had health and dental insurance for Janiece in addition to paying child support, so for her not to receive all the money he pays is ridiculous. James has been paying child support through the system ever since Janiece was three years old and before that he met every need and want the child could have ever thought she may have wanted and or needed.

At some point in one of our many court hearings we found out that James had an arrearage child support case. Apparently when he first started paying court ordered child support for Janiece, Monica (unbeknownst to James) had been receiving benefits from the state which meant he had to pay that money back.

Now James had an attachment on his check for that amount too. A child should be able to get the benefits of the best of what both parents has to offer. Janiece missed out on what we had to offer because her mom could not get *past the bitterness*.

Blurred Lines

"Do not pray for an easy life, pray for the strength to endure a difficult one."
-Bruce Lee

Don't get me wrong, James never wanted to shake his responsibility for Janiece. He was not only there for this child financially; he took care of her as well. I wonder did she report *that* to the agency. Do you think these agencies ever ask for moms to pay any of this type of money back or at the very least ask them to split it? While they are getting his money out of each check, she is running him back and forth to court every chance she gets out of pure aggravation and taunting him because her check is late. Because the State is backed up or short staffed, payments fall between the cracks and James has to keep taking off work to go to court.

The courts see the arrearage and would not allow him to explain the case or show the paperwork from the last case that they gave him which explained what happened. They tell him they are going to leave it up to Monica to decide between locking him up on a $500 bail or let him go and he could pay it later. Of course she chose to have him locked up.

That didn't make sense to me. Locking him up doesn't serve a purpose because if he is locked up, he can't work and if he can't work she doesn't get any money. That told me another thing about her - she just wanted him to hurt for something. I went to the bank and bailed my husband out within the hour! You bitter bitty!

Now that wouldn't be the last time she pulled him into court. I can remember another time she pulled him in and after hearing her go back and forth about this and that, the Judge just ordered James to hire an *attorney ad Litem* for Janiece. Before our hearing the attorney met with Monica and I and witnessed a scene. She totally lost it on me.

"You are one stupid m***** f*****," She leaned forward to say to me.

I sat there in stunned silence. Who behaves this way in public – in a courtroom and in front of an attorney.

"You will never replace me," Monica continued and slapped the table hard.

This was all so ridiculous to me. I was not used to this type of behavior. She appeared almost insane!

What also stunned me was that the attorney ad litem just sat there and allowed her to come apart at the seams at my expense while he simply looked on in disbelief. Finally, I'd had enough. I was horrified at what was happening or may have happened in that tiny room.

"I refuse to sit here and take this type of abuse from anyone," I said. "Please excuse me." I walked quickly to the hallway where James was waiting.

"Why was Monica yelling like that?" He asked with clear concern.

I couldn't even talk. I was so angry and I knew that if I spoke, I would cry so I just waved my hand and he knew to give me some time to calm down.

The one good thing that came from this is that the attorney saw that Monica was totally bitter about James moving on without her. She was upset that I was in the picture and all of this back and forth stuff with the courts was only about that and had nothing to do with Janiece.

He did let the judge know that we were not the problem and how a lot of this was stemming from Monica's hostility.

The attorney met with the judge and after what seemed like hours, we were in front of the judge who was giving James more time and telling Monica to basically move on.

The judge also instructed Monica to not talk about us in front of Janiece and told her she needed to move on. She was hot. James got a little more time added to his visitations which bothered her even more. The attorney ad litem saw what he needed to see I guess.

But I wish he really would have talked to Janiece in a different setting and visited both homes. This wouldn't be the last time our family dealt with *blurred lines*.

God Had Other Plans

> "We may encounter defeats, but we must not be defeated."
> **-Maya Angelou**

Visitations should have gotten better from this point but they didn't. Fridays were still the same, but we just adapted I guess. Saturdays were wonderful. Sundays were dreadful because Janiece did not want to go home.

She began doing little things that we never understood. For starters, Janiece would say hurtful things to her sister Janelle and then tell us that her mom told her to do it.

We knew Janiece adored Janelle – that was undeniable, so we were certain Monica was behind all of that. The woman was relentless in her meanness.

She sent Janiece to our house one Christmas with a gift for Janelle, but nothing for Jason and her explanation was simply, "Jason ain't my brother."

Jason is her brother and whether her mom wants to accept this huge fact or not doesn't make it untrue.

Summers were great! Janiece went to the same camps that Jason went to, participated in whatever he participated in and then some. Monica felt like Janiece should not be in camps. She said her time was supposed to be with James not held up in camps.

The phone calls started back with a vengeance. They were very hateful, bitter calls. Some of them were from kids calling me bitches and whatnot. But the one that I will never ever get out of my head is the one that I knew exactly where it came from. I was talking 'woman to woman' - or so I thought - to Monica early one afternoon. I thought we were making headway towards some sort of peace agreement. She had something totally different on her mind I guess.

"I know you're trying to take Janiece away from me," She said with venom.

"I would never do that," I replied. "I'm just looking for a way for all of us to coexist and co-parent."

"You need to just mind your own freaking business," she said with more anger than ever. "You'll be dead soon anyway with your sick ass. And with any luck you'll pass that illness on to your daughter!"

I looked at the phone and was like, "What the what?" Now WHO in their RIGHT mind thinks or says some crap like that? I have Lupus and now many other illnesses because of the Lupus and I wouldn't wish it on my worst enemy. I was floored when she said this because she has two children of her own that were born with some major medical disadvantages, so as a mother how could you wish something on another child. Let me just say that NOW all I can do is pray for her, but THEN I was hanging up the phone and calling my ride or die sister and was like, "Let's go do this!" But thankfully, *God had other plans.*

Like Nothing Happened

> "Darkness cannot drive out darkness:
> only light can do that.
> Hate cannot drive out hate:
> only love can do that."
> **-Martin Luther King**

I managed to calm down before doing anything stupid, but I was still angry with James because the only way Monica could have known something so personal about me was if he had told her. However, I knew deep down that he probably told her that because he and I both kept thinking that by talking to her and letting her in that we would win her over and she would stop being so evil and ornery.

In the heat of things though it didn't stop me from going off on him about his ignorant baby momma and all her drama. I was upset and hurt. She kicked me where it hurt the most. She bought my baby into this and wished a horrible disease over her that is life altering and debilitating. How was I supposed to deal with that? I was spinning.

I would be lying if I said I didn't start second guessing all of my decisions to this point. Should I have pursued this relationship after she warned me to walk away? She told me out of her own mouth that I would regret it if I didn't. She told me my life would be hell as long as she had had a daughter with him and Janiece is undeniably James's daughter. I was thinking, "What have I gotten myself into?" James and I somewhat went back and forth about her comments to me. He felt I shouldn't even entertain her foolishness and should just let it go and ignore her. I felt that was so easy for him because she was usually only pointing her anger towards *me* with venom.

I always wonder if he realizes that she is only keeping his daughter away from him, because he is not with her. If he dropped me today or tomorrow they would be back friends - *laughing, heheeheeeing* and *chopping it up like nothing happened;* if he allowed it.

A Bigger Issue

> "The truth is,
> everyone is going to hurt you.
> You just got to find the ones
> worth suffering for."
> **-Bob Marley**

Over the next few years, things remained hostile. They never got better. We attended more court dates, parenting classes and James and I even sought out help groups on our own. It was ridiculous. One counselor gave us some insight.

"When you share a child and the hate and dysfunction is this great, you are tormenting the child. The child is taught and programmed to have several personalities."

In essence she was saying that we (all of us) were teaching Janiece to have schizophrenia behavior. We were expecting her to abide by our rules and be respectful regardless to what her mother told her to do.

Imagine only having a child in your home every other weekend and having to debug them of garbage on Friday, having a beautiful day Saturday and half of Sunday and then on Sunday afternoon when she realizes it is close to the time to return to her momma she turns into a monster or just starts crying saying she doesn't want to go back. I understood what the counselor was saying.

No matter how hard James tried to talk to Monica it turned into a big battle. She accused me of doing all kinds of things to Janiece like spanking her, not feeding her, combing her hair wrong and even not liking her. It was ridiculous.

I have never ever spanked Janiece. Not that I didn't want to, but the situation was bad enough without adding corporal punishment. This was hard for me because I have always been the type of parent that if your kid was with me, your kid was treated just like one of mine! If my kids were jumping on the bed and I warned them about jumping on the bed and my kid got a spanking for continuing to jump on the bed, then guess what - your kid got a spanking for jumping on the bed too. No exception.

However, Janiece got special rules in our home because of the uniqueness of circumstances. I think if I had so much as tapped her hand her mom would have had me under the jail if she could of. So the most I have ever did with her is raise my voice and sent her to James.

Sending her to James was like sending her to the chocolate factory! James is a push over when it came to discipline really. All the kids know this. His bark is worse than his bite. And because he didn't get to see Janiece like he really wanted to, he thought he could make up for it by letting her get away with more. Now everyone knows in hindsight that this only creates *a bigger issue* down the line.

Food for Thought

"There is no greater agony
than bearing an untold story
inside of you."
-Maya Angelou

Blending my family was something that I thought was going to be effortless. James and I were in love and our children were young. They got along and seemed to genuinely love each other as well. My family loved Janiece as if I had given birth to her myself. No one treated her any differently than any of my other children. Until reading this book, many won't know she is not biologically mine - that is how much I vowed to make sure I blended my family.

I was never going to use the words *step* and or *half siblings* in my home. We are a family and that is just it. We are one unit. To me, *step* or *half* is division. I never wanted division in my home. Surprisingly, that is exactly what I have. After years of torment and torture Monica has won. She has beaten us down. I feel like we - James and I - need to separate so that he can be a part of Janiece's life.

We are now years into this and Monica has not let up one bit, but I'm broken. I feel destroyed. I often wonder is there now going to be two more kids, Jason and Janelle, added to the list of kids who are living apart from their father. Only in my case it won't be because James and I can't get along, it will be because Monica has divided the family and I can no longer tolerate the headaches, torture and all the back and forth.

The one thing I know for sure though is that if we go our separate ways, James will be a part of Jason and Janelle lives without a problem. I just no longer will have the headache of having to deal with Monica. I really have to do some serious thinking on this. I love my family and would hate to have to dismantle it all because of the hatred of some miserable person constantly causing havoc but this is getting out of hand. I am beginning to fear someone is going to get hurt. Actually, someone has already been hurt.

Food for thought.

Epilogue

The impact the struggle with Monica caused on our family was far reaching. All of our children; Jason, Janiece and Janelle were hurt of course, but more than that they were confused by it all.

Janiece was at our home a lot and for the most part when she was there, we all got along – until she wasn't there. The kids nor I understood how she could be so happy one day and seem to hate us all the next. I realized early on that her mom had a lot to do with her behaving the way she did, but that didn't make it hurt any less.

I couldn't explain what wasn't rational to me as an adult to our minor children.

My marriage suffered the most I think. James and I spent a lot of time talking or bickering over the situation. The mere subject of Janiece was a sore topic in our household. He felt torn between being there for his daughter and comforting me. It was like to do one or the other meant leaving someone out. I got it, but again, that didn't make it hurt any less.

In my mind, I felt like this should be easy – Janiece was loved by all involved – so, let's love her and raise her together. End of discussion. Apparently, it wasn't that easy.

I was diagnosed with Lupus in 1994 and one thing that causes me to have flare-ups is stress so you can imagine how my health deteriorated because of what I considered nonsense.

It felt like if I wasn't arguing with Monica, in a heated debate with James, comforting our children or explaining things to my family; I was in the hospital or at the Doctor's office trying to find some relief from my symptoms. It was all too much!

Many times I wanted to separate myself from James. Not because I didn't love him or wanted our marriage to work, but simply to have some peace and quiet. Of course James would never consent to that – so we continued to discuss it.

Talking to James was hard because like me, he was too close to the situation. Often times I closed myself off in my room and didn't talk to anyone. I just stayed in my bed, took my medication and/or just slept.

I prayed a lot and I also talked to my mom and my sister about the situation. They were supportive and didn't try to influence me one way or the other. They knew how much I loved James and how badly I wanted our families to blend.

I've been asked by many if knowing what I know now, would I make the same choice to marry James.

I continue to ask myself that question.

Book Club Discussion

Can families truly blend? Have you seen it done successfully?

Have you experienced drama at the hands of an ex-spouse or significant other?

How do you think children feel underneath the weight of blending?

Should couples attempt to blend or keep their lives separate when possible?

What can courts do to make blending easier?

What can we as women do to make blending easier?

What should men do to make blending easier?

Hindsight is always 20/20. In this story, do you see red flags?

Is love truly unconditional?

Book Club Discussion

Parents say they want what's best for their child(ren). Is blending when it doesn't work, best for the child(ren)?

Why do you think women often blame the new woman/wife for the end of a relationship?

Why is the anger directed more at the new woman/wife and not so much towards the man?

After reading this story, does it cause you to think about making changes in your own life? If so, what?

If you have attempted blending, if you had it to do all over again – would you?

Is love worth a life filled with hate?

Would you give up a love for the sake of peace?

How do you successfully discipline blended family children?

About the Author

Author Angie Johnson's parents are from the south. They took their children 'down south' often and in the process managed to instill in their children all the southern values they learned from their own childhood.

Loving and helping children is what Angie loves most. As a girl scout leader for nearly six years and as well as a classroom/library assistant Angie was able to surround herself with children while giving them the support and encouragement they sometimes lacked. Her and her husband have opened their home to provide a safe haven for many babies and kids.

Angie is a loving wife, stay-at-home mom and helps raise her grandson. She currently resides in Midwest Missouri with her husband, son, youngest daughter and grandson.

"The future depends on what we do in the present."
-Mahatma Gandhi

Contact

Butterfly Typeface Publishing
for all your
publishing & writing needs!

Iris M Williams
PO Box 56193
Little Rock AR 72215
www.butterflytypeface.com